Bioluminescence

Karen Richards

Copyright © 2025 Karen Richards

All rights reserved. No part of this publication including the cover image may be reproduced, distributed, or transmitted in any form or by any means, without the prior written permission of the publisher.

Cover Photography: Deni Cupit

Cover Design: Islam Farid

ISBN: 978-0-6489919-4-6

Foreword

When I first saw the image of Bioluminescence on my amazing mate, Deni's Instagram page, I knew it would be the cover for this book, because truly, what sums life up more perfectly than being able to find the ethereal in the most unexpected places, to realise that finding something so incredibly illuminating in the darkness can show us how the light that we emit in our hardest times can also be seen as beautiful and powerful in someone else's eyes.

Bioluminescence really sums up this collection of poetry, shining light on love, hope, hurt and healing. You can succumb to the darkness or find hope and beauty in the words that follow, it is for you to choose, just please remember the darkest night always comes before the dawn.

CONTENTS

Celestial Sparks	9
Tides of Mourning Light	45
Funeral of Dusk	93
Glimpses from the Abyss	139
Luminous Hearts	175

Celestial Sparks

Wonder of Wild

We collapsed into
September's arms,
another fallen winter
lying catatonic on our skin,
a season of tears,
soaking through the earth,
beneath new beginnings
of a lilac spring canopy.

This is not mourning;
this is heavenly purification
for broken souls
who have stood toe to toe
with death and found life
in the radiance of rebellion
and the wonder of wild.

Our feminine awakening
has *begun.*

Comfort

It's been a while; please forgive me for the days I wandered past wildflowers, lost in the humdrum of bustling city streets, where the sun's warmth felt distant and the wind whispered unheard.

I return whole now to the quiet of the forest, where our earth exhales softly, and leaves tell the story of seasons change and lingering moments.

Here, among roots and shadows, I find long-forgotten comfort - a reminder that even in our absence, the world halts in silence, patiently awaiting our return.

Spring is...

As August gives way to September
there is a love letter
being written in my soul,
the black ink landing softer
onto ancient parchment
than it once did.

Purple wisteria climbs the corners,
wrapping itself around me
in every way I long to be held.

Maybe spring is hope,
is softness, is forgiveness;
maybe it is the home
I've been yearning for.

One thing I do know, even now:
this love letter is your gift.
Keep it well, keep it safe,
keep it long after
these seasons have passed,
with all my love.

Lavish Linguistics

He speaks in
unfamiliar tongues,
lavish linguistics
of lips I long to kiss,
pressing the warmth
of his touch
to a heart that is his,
to protect evermore
in the palm of his hands.

Umber and Gold

Burnt umber and gold
cast shadows against your smile;
it never takes more
than a whisper of autumn
to fall for you once more.

Things that Keep Me Warm

The flicker of wild flame in your eyes / the honeyed taste of your lips on mine / your fingertips dancing along my spine / the way your brow furrows when you tell me you miss me / how your lips linger against my forehead as you fall asleep / the warmth in your voice when you speak my name / the rhythmic serenade of your heart as I rest my head on your chest / whispered promises in the dead of night / the way you look at me, as if a universe exists in my eyes / the softness in the way you cradle me in your arms / and how you always feel like home.

Hush of Dusk

Find me at the hush of dusk, where shadows unfurl and the sky melts into hues of deep indigo. Hear the twilight's whisper singing lullabies as sleepy stars blink shyly, hesitant to join the dance.

Lie with me in the grass, the scent of earth rising, while silhouettes of leaves stretch lazily across our bodies. Watch the gum tree branches cradle the last sigh of light, moonlight spilling like silver silk across our skin.

Notice how the world inhales deeply, wrapped in velvety night, as crickets serenade the closing day, their song a soothing balm.

Feel, in this tranquility, time pausing - inviting our hearts to explore this easily forgotten gift of peace.

Soft Surrender

My fingertips remember your skin's soft surrender - the warmth of every curve, and the way the candlelight trembled, a faint hesitation, before settling into the contours of your body.

My touch lingered, tracing the paths it had memorised: the slope of your hip, the hollow of your collarbone, and the constellation of freckles on your shoulder shining like a map to secret places.

As the flames dwindled and darkness drew near, our outlines blurred in its gentle creep.

Finally, as the candles burned low, those shadows, they swallowed us whole.

Fragile Hour

Let us linger in this hush of inevitable dawn, holding time as golden rays stretch and fade against the softness of our waking slumber.

Watch in wonder as blushing horizons offer us promises of unfathomable joy, while we fight the urge to retreat into the shadows, to the dark of night that belongs to only us, free of this unspoken ache as parting draws near.

It is in this fragile hour, thick with the taste of mournful goodbye, that too soon you will be gone, and empty sheets will be all that remain to cradle the ribbons of dying light.

Anywhere but Here

Let's go somewhere - anywhere but here.

Let's slip through the cracks of daylight,
hearts racing, hand in hand, climb mountains,
shedding our inhibitions to the dawn.

Let the light kiss our skin,
breathe life into our weary bones.

Let's forge a world of our own,
one that forgets the past.

Yes, let's go somewhere, anywhere but here.

Fortress

You cracked the spine
of my fortress
lifted the bricks
of my trauma
and placed them
on your chest
until your breaths
were little more than wisps
in the chill of dawn.

And so you were buried,
a hero of my heart.

Love Me Anyway

Love me anyway, from the hollow of my imperfections to the places where shadows stretch and jagged scars reside, where I bury the crushing weight of unvoiced terrors, and the doubts that creep like evening rain.

Love me in the fissures of my battered soul, where sadness and loneliness gather and the last embers fade.

Love me in the moments I am fractured and unholy, when only splintered shards of me remain.

Love me even in the haunting beauty of the tangled mess I've made.

Love me anyway, though I am unfinished, a story;
with an ending yet unclaimed.

Revelation

Time teaches us to notice the smallest shifts, how shadows stretch across the forest floor, how the air thickens with the scent of petrichor, how the earth holds its breath before the storm.

We see the slow unfurling of petals, colour revealed in patience, branches twisting toward the light, while hollowed bark seals over old wounds. Transformation is quiet, often unnoticed until the bloom breaks free.

In the rustle of grass beneath our feet, we feel the weight of seasons, the gentle exhale of autumn leaves, a tender farewell reminding us to hold beauty lightly, knowing it is fleeting.

My Love

Batten down the hatches a storm is coming. Prepare yourself for a hurricane, for love unlike any you have known.

Take shelter in the eye of the storm when you can, in the reprieve of the rare calm that sweeps through and reminds you what love is meant to feel like.

Get comfortable with silence. Embrace it. Mould it into unforgettable moments. Speak her words back to her - turn them into prophecy, a promise, a forever – and do what no one has ever done before: stay.

A Beautiful Life

He sees himself as old,
in a fractured distortion
of unworthy reflection.
But I see those lines
as a roadmap,
guiding me through
every happiness
that ever travelled
the curve of his smile
to the crease of his eyes
leaving behind
a permanent reminder
of a beautiful life.

All I can hope,
when he looks in the mirror,
is that he remembers
some of those lines
were carved with love
by me.

Surrender

We were lying side by side, hand in hand, on pillows of soft white sand. Breath knocked from our lungs as we spluttered and gasped for a semblance of life - drenched and shivering, clothes clinging to bare skin, trembling beneath the final glow of day, salt glistening against us.

We've been here before, you and I, in the aftermath of a storm, its fury spent, wreckage drifting out to sea, leaving only the debris of us on the shore.

Yet these days, we've somehow learned to survive what once threatened to break us - holding hands as we float and surrender.

The Whisper of Your Touch

In the meantime,
let me rest here,
against the cadence
of your chest.

Lowered lashes
teeter on the cusp
of sleep.

Your fingertips
flicker like embers
along my spine,
lips a gentle ache
upon my brow.

Please, just stay
a little while longer,
before only the whisper
of your touch remains.

Salvation – haiku

when love falls apart
your precious heartstrings hold me
my one salvation

Somehow

Somehow, I dream us back here,
to a place in time where love balances
on a knife's edge of sunshine,
yet still we suffocate in the chasm of grey,
desolation raining onto the earth below.

Somehow, I dream us back here,
to the place in time
we burned into ash upon the tide,
giving and taking every grain of love from the shore,
only to lose it in the vastness of heartache.

Somehow, I dream us back here,
to two hopeless and wounded halves
of a complicated love
uncertain whether the ending will change.

All I know is somehow,
I found you dreaming us back here too -
and maybe this time that's enough.

Your Name – haiku

they tear from within
that which beats for only you
hearts last gasp: your name

4 a.m.

It's 4 a.m. and I am awake again, watching shadows of streetlights dance across my wall, feeling you lost in another night, in another place and time.

Somehow, our sleeplessness aligns with the stars above. Maybe we're both chasing the same dream or fleeing the same thoughts, connected only by this wakeful ache.

Please know I will wait with you until dawn breaks, where we can linger in anticipation of a reunion beneath these all-too-unfamiliar stars.

If I Knew Where it Hurt

If I knew where it hurt, I would beg for the softness of your lips to soothe it away, whisper to your fingertips all that remains scarred, so you could trace their path.

I'd let your voice be the balm to calm my storm - even when we both know this hurt is only a shadow, with no beginning or end. Just a pause, where I learn the silence of pain can only be found in your arms.

Ache

These months pass me by, and I wait. I wait for the ache in my heart to subside, for this yearning to swallow you whole, the way you have unwittingly consumed me.

But this love never leaves, it only grows and grows, until there is no space for anything, or anyone else but you - until your pain, your sadness, your heartache seep into my soul, and I can no longer speak without your name resting softly on my lips.

Love Never Really Dies

Love never really dies.
It simply hides
in the creases of our skin,
in the silence between the lines
of a well-worn book,
in the soft give
of your favourite sweater.

It lingers in nostalgia's ache,
in the warmth of a fading touch,
a ghost of what we had
haunting the edges
of what we always wished
could have been.

Heart for Sale

This heart is for sale, but I warn you - it is now just a canvas of cracks and chasms. Still, it beats with a ferocity that defies its fragility.

It's a paradox, really. The more it breaks, the more it learns to love. Not in spite of the pain, but because of it.

Its scars do not diminish its capacity; they amplify it. The veins become conduits - for love, for connection, for the messy, beautiful chaos that is me.

Wait, so you're willing to take on all of its brokenness?

Then I'll give it to you - free.

Before the Trauma

I grieve who you would have become
without the trauma.

Before glass butterflies
laid lifelessly on the windowsill
refracting every shade of blue
and casting them into your heart.

Before the dots and dashes
of scars whispered an SOS in Morse code
to every predator who left their lies
between your thighs.

Before grief found a home
between your fourth and fifth rib,
ripping the very fabric
of your blood-stained shirt,
which reeked of death
and became your white flag.

Before you sought softness
in everything hard,
strength in every weakness,
life in the shadow of death.

I grieve the woman
you would have become
without the trauma -
but I am proud of the woman
you are.

Undiscovered World

There is an undiscovered world
living beneath the surface of my skin
where harmony and peace
drift like a soft summer breeze,
whispering hidden secrets
against pale cheeks,
kissing them with
nothing more
than a breath of warmth.

Quietly I fold thoughts
into poetry, penned
with a hint of hope,
with a fragile weight of healing,
and with that
all-too-familiar longing
for home.

Poet

I love you in the only way
a poet ever could -
with sonnets cupped
gently in open palms
a wind of words
settling softly onto blank pages,
laid to rest for eternity
within the hollow of my chest
where the heart
of a poet once lived.

Goddess

My head is filled
with ocean song
as I am baptised
in sea-whispers,
ripples of waves
kissing my skin,
anointing me
goddess of the sea.

I am adrift in the swell
of acceptance,
somewhere deep
in cobalt blue.

Remind Me

Autumn, remind me of your beauty, the gentle shift which offers me, a single clutch of much-needed warmth from the egg-yolk sun as it retreats into a sky, painted with brazen twilight. Shadows stretch long and lazy, reaching eager ears, whispering of the cold to come.

The scent of earth lingers, mingling with smoke from hearthside fires. And in this stillness, I find comfort. Here beauty dwells in change, in the quiet strength of decay, where every ending becomes a promise of beginning, and fallen leaves are but a descent toward something new.

Ethereal Embrace

Between the tender sigh
of newborn freesia,
winter drifts into slumber
and spring awakens.

Emerald leaves
bow beneath the weight
of a zephyr's kiss
surrendering freely
to the season's call.

Soft unfolding of hope
rise with innocent abandon

I whisper, "*take me with you*",
into the open arms
of Mother Nature's ethereal embrace
she purrs her reply -
"*You are home, darling child.
You are home*".

Wispy Sapling

They liken me
to a fragile sapling,
roots flailing,
searching for a place to grow.

Yet they forget the sapling
is rebirth,
a seedling fallen
from ancient bough.

And I grow stronger
with each descent,
my heart open,
my will unbroken,
ready once more
to live again.

Tides of Mourning Light

Raindrops

Raindrops die
in the palm
of my hand.

Can nothing I love
survive the fall?

Tremor

Sometimes, I feel
like the slight tremor
of a steady hand,
barely visible
to the naked eye,
until a glass shatters
and people begin searching
for someone
to shoulder the blame
for the mess they've made.

Courage

I'm not crying; my words are.
They spill as ink across pages,
leaving behind indents - love letters to you.

I have become nothing more
than a vessel for my heart,
confessing too late,
all I never found the courage to say.

Demons and Doubt

I spend too much time inside my own head,
where demons whisper and doubts are fed.

A prison of thoughts, a cell of my making
no key, no freedom, just a lifetime of aching.

Dear Life,

We need to talk about your expectations. Enough is enough. My shoulders are fractured beneath the weight of your relentless demands, the burden of *"you are never given more than you can carry."* I carry the salt of tears shed in your wake; each drop a testament to my struggle.

When I beg for a break, it is not a plea for more heartbreak. When I tell you I can't take anymore, I do not mean love, or fleeting glimpses of joy, those rare sparks that fuel me.

But you twist my words in cruel ways. My pleas become sins, my cries for help mistaken for selfishness and cowardice, when all I have ever asked is to leave in peace, to find solace away from this unyielding weight.

I remember laughter with friends, the warmth of the sun on my face, the quiet wonder of a starry night. These moments are lifelines, yet too often overshadowed by your demands.

Let me escape this. Grant me the peace I seek, not as surrender, but as a reward for my humanity, that refuses to break.

Another Life

Maybe in another life, we would sit together, bodies pressed close, your trembling hand clasped tightly in mine as you bury a friend. I would hold you to my chest, absorbing each sigh of sorrow, as love learns to endure the distance between heaven and earth.

Maybe in another life, words for the eulogy would be left unspoken, and you would let the touch along your spine guide your gaze from grief to the quiet assurance in my eyes - a hazel harbour in which to hide.

Maybe in another life, we could rewrite the stars, reshape our fate. But in this one, I remain only a whisper - a haunting specter in your storm, always wishing to bridge the space between us. To be your solace. To be the love that endures. To be the love that might one day make you whole.

Emergency

In the event of an emergency, meet my gaze.
Drink in every inch of me one last time,
brush the tears from my cheeks as you feign belief
in the brittle bravado of my crumbling soul.

Show me your pounding heart,
your trembling hands, your unsteady breath,
then turn away.

Let our silence in the eye of the storm
fall into the chasm of swallowed hope,
and surrender yourself to the reality
that when you look back,
you will see I am not following.

Find solace in my absence,
but do not mourn what is, what was,
or what will never be.

Instead, remember my love
as an anchor, a tether to forever,
where I remain yours for eternity.

Two Solitudes

If the moon had never loved the stars,
we'd be splinters, adrift
in the vast, unbridgeable void,
lost to the night's embrace.

Perhaps we would never find
the sky that binds us,
nor see our longing mirrored
in the celestial dance above.

In darkness, we would remain
two solitudes, starlight apart,
each a universe unto itself,
unlit, unnamed, unknown.

The Taste

When your lips touch mine,
is it bitterness you taste?
The ghosts of thoughts
that have haunted me,
of words that have sat
atop my tongue for far too long,
dancing like fire,
but afraid to ignite.

Do they taste of regret,
of things left unsaid,
truths swaddled in the gauze of hesitation,
edges frayed with wear,
air thick with what could have been,
if only our courage had bloomed.

Proof

I would hate it
if the only proof
of my love
were the scars
I left behind.

Unravelling Time

We captured the night, the moon, with its silvery tendrils of light cupped between our outstretched palms, a fortune teller of the stars' reflection we found dancing in each other's eyes.

If only time could unravel back to that night, when two hearts discovered all they could ever need, save for the lies that remain untold.

Louder

In the stillness of night,
a heavy breath lingers.

Unspoken words drape like shadows,
clinging ghost-like to the walls,
an echo of history.

Silence, a weight, a quiet ache,
fills the emptiness between heartbeats,
the distant murmur of rain
whispers memories long since hushed,
reminding me that absence
always speaks louder than love.

Lost

I think we're lost; our words no longer find their place in the silence as they once did, thoughts now faltering mid-air like sentences, scattered in the chaos as we drift apart.

I am left to wonder if we have simply become two people who've outgrown the poetry we once wrote together, if the ink has simply faded from the page, or if the rhythm of our love still lingers in the lines, waiting for the right words to rekindle the flame.

Kindred Spirit

I tore a hole in the moon
to see if darkness
could heal her
open wounds.

Instead, I found
a kindred spirit,
addicted to
and in love
with the pain.

Slipping Away

One day,
they will find my body
at the edge
of the ocean's ebb,
fingers splayed
upon grains of sand,
in a desperate bid
to keep just one thing
from slipping away.

Anxiety

Your messages linger in my mind; a constant stream of worst-case scenarios left at 3 a.m. When darkness amplifies every fear, you whisper my name, convince me of my unworthiness, and I am drawn back into your vortex.

Your tone is urgent, leaving me in a perpetual state of emergency. I am expected to respond, to calm the rising panic, but the words get stuck in my throat, and I am left to replay our encounter over and over, endlessly searching for a way out.

Bomb Shelter

I folded every poem
I wrote for you
like origami,
hoping to build
a bomb shelter
for your heart,

But I have since realised
the futility of such a task
for words
are not shelter enough
to protect you
from me.

Reckless Abandon

How mighty is thy sword
when driven with reckless abandon
into the most tender of hearts.

Chandelier

Tears hang as
crystalline chandeliers
in a forest,
refracting light from pain,
blinding stars,
until they fall
like neon bullets,
slaughtering the souls
seeking salvation
before dawn.

Bruised Butterflies

We stopped holding hands,
the void between our fingertips
spreading like wildfire
to our lips, our hips,
and our hearts.

There was no turning back,
no filling the emptiness
we had grown accustomed
to creating.

There was no saving each other
from the bruised butterflies
of love.

Cupid

If only I had known when I met you
that Cupid would lay his bow
at Venus' feet
and walk away from love.

Perhaps we should have too,
before this ache
became all we had
to remember each other by.

Matching Wounds

We wear matching wounds, subtle contours beneath our skin, a geography of hurt mapped by choice and chance.

We linger in the spaces where words fall short, where the air is thick with what remains unspoken, yet understood.

In quieter moments, we trace the outlines of our scars, not for comfort, but for the familiarity of a silence that has become a wound that never quite heals.

Dust of Blame

The weight of our love's collapse
settles in my bones.

Dust of blame,
not mine to claim,
invades my lungs
and steals my last breath.

I crumble,
forever the rubble of another.

Insomniac's Dawn

I live my life awaiting the insomniac's dawn,
that first peek of light from the sun's sleeping eyes,
filtering through cracks in the blinds
warming the heart of my loneliness,
bringing a fragile silence to the darkness's cruel truth.

Some wounds weep only for the night.

Shooting Star

Watching you leave
felt like the final spark
of a shooting star.

What once blazed bright
and beautiful
fizzled into nothingness,
leaving my heart
a desolate landscape
of ash and debris.

Unto Me

God once chose
to gift you words
when He dipped
your heart in ink.

But unto me
He gifted the
white nothingness
of parchment,
and I have grown tired
of existing solely
to be that onto
which you bleed.

Haunting

I wonder if it haunts you, the unearned ease in your step, the way you move through life with laughter as a shield, while I stitch together pieces of a shattered trust.

I wonder if you still recall the weight of your gaze, the kindness you twisted into something more, as I linger in this nightmare, a ghost of the girl I once was, lost in the fog of your indifference. Meanwhile, you weave stories to cloak your truth, no one noticing the fraying seams, the disconnect, the way you play the hero in a tale where you have only ever been the villain.

I wonder if it haunts you, the knowledge that each day I rise from the smoldering ruin of your choices, in quiet rebellion. And though you may forget my name, my face, my existence, I am the keeper of my flame, and you will only ever live in the ashes of those remains.

How to Stem the Bleeding

Learn to cauterise your own wounds first / apply enough gauze to mummify the moon / wrap your body around mine to stop me bleeding out / find one single vein of self-love in either of us to begin the transfusion / instead of stitches, use that thread to sew closed the lips of those who use their words to wound / know that there is nothing you can do to save someone whose soul you didn't even break.

Broken Poets

Broken people call themselves poets,
for there is no more powerful way
to convey pain
than to pull your still beating heart
straight from your chest
and place it on the page
for the world to see.

Tracing Silhouettes

Your absence has become a palpable thing: the memory of your fingertips brushing against the hollow of my chest, the feather-like softness of your whispers resting in the crook of my neck.

Nights blend together in a haze of loneliness, each one just more of the same. I still feel your skin's warmth against my cheek, the gentle thrum of your heartbeat rocking me to sleep, your sighs sweeping like a soft breeze through my hair.

But you are no longer here, and I am left another night tracing your silhouette onto empty sheets.

The Words You Didn't Say

After all these years, I am still finding the words you didn't say, hidden in plain view, still searching for the reason you left without a sound.

Sometimes I think I've found you in the lyric of a song, a quote in a book, or in the poetry I write, but truthfully, you were gone long before you left.

I am tired of focusing on the why when my heart already knows the answer… why not.

Wounded Animal

Trauma left me
gift-wrapped
in crippling anxiety,
tied with bows
of barbed wire.

While you tiptoe
through landmines
of hidden triggers
and sharp edges,
trying not to wake
the wounded animal within,
we are both left scared,
scarred and bleeding
from wounds
neither of us caused.

Violet

The violets whisper
some nonsense
about beauty being found
even in the throes of tragedy,
but I am too busy
remembering the way their shade
once marked my skin,
and how I am yet
to find beauty in the pain.

Abandoned

You've always felt like a shadow,
as close as anyone could ever be.

But the truth is in the darkness,
you're the one who abandons me.

Irony

You'll be happy to know
that after the fall I learnt to fly.

The irony is
the meaninglessness of it all,
now there is no one to witness
me leave this all behind.

Linger

In my dreams, I still see you.

Of course, I know it's you
by the way my heart aches,
where the shadows of you
still linger.

Grief (Tercet)

In the still of dusk, where shadows confide,
Grief carves its path like a relentless tide,
Each heartbeat a ghost we cannot hide.

We Fell

We fell, a gentle rustle letting go of all that had shaped us, loved us, embraced us as we grew, all that had witnessed our transformation from nothing into a cherished turning of season.

If only we had known that in doing so, we would become our undoing, crumpling and dying beneath the warmth of an autumn sun, our hues now memories, faded.

Everything has a season, and ours surrendered to the fall, in neatly raked piles of leaves at the turning of burnt copper and gold.

Lighthouse

I have come to realise
I find comfort
in the way strangers
shelter from their storms
in the unlived spaces within me,
for it means that, despite my darkness,
the lighthouse in me
still shines brightly enough
for others to find safe harbour
on their journey home.

Gatherer

I was born a gatherer.

I collect people, memories,
and unnecessary things,
always arranging and shuffling them
into beautiful displays,
making sure I don't misplace
anyone or anything.

Accumulating grief and trauma,
however, is easier.

But no matter how I try to
stuff them both into suitcases
and send them on their way,
uncannily, they seem to be
the only things that stay.

Peace in the Pieces

Someday
I will surrender
to the pain,
tear the ribbons
of stray thoughts
from my head,
and rewrite
my story
over and over
on my skin,
until I can find
some semblance
of peace
in the pieces.

Ancient Pulse

The forest is quiet,
the trees standing
like sentinels
in the stillness.

A bird calls,
but its song
is swallowed
by the silence.

Sap slows
in the trees' veins,
their ancient pulse
faltering.

In the chasm
of swallowed hope,
the darkness
is absolute.

Escape Artist

The bars of this cage leave imprinted lines on my skin, metal biting until the pressure wears welts into my tender fragility. My body is now a canvas for the art of confinement, brittle and bloodied, with fingers grasping through the blazing, red-hot steel, summoning help that never arrives.

Somehow, still, I muster the strength of every ghost whose trauma holds me hostage. I use it to pry apart the rusted shackles, slip through the cracks of my own mind, and evolve into an escape artist of the unstoppable kind.

Coffin

This poem is a coffin,
lined with words so heavy
they require no funeral,
no fanfare, no eulogy.

They have come to know
their darkness so well
that this coffin,
it buries itself.

Funeral of Dusk

Ending in Y

I don't love myself; in truth, I can barely even like myself on days that end in "y".

Each day, I face my reflection, straining to catch even a glimpse of the beauty you insist lives in me. But I find no kindness in the crease of my eyes, no courage in the faded scars etched across my skin, and no tenderness in the quiet purse of my lips.

Perhaps it is the shattered mirror I peer through - cracked, distorted, that leaves me scattered in fragments; pieces shaped to show you what I wish you'd believe, yet never enough to make me believe it too.

Little Ray of Sunshine

I was born a little ray of sunshine,
an open-chested beam of light
that tore a hole through the sky
and landed in the belly
of a copper-hued autumn.

There was no way I could have foreseen
the all-consuming darkness,
the drawn-out melancholy
of the long winter ahead,
not until you left,
not until you stole the rhythm
from my heart and turned it
into a beat to walk away to.

Until you bled me dry
of the liquid amber
that made me who I was,
and used it to fuel
your own happiness
in a world without me.

Brutality

Sometimes all that survives is our willingness to surrender to the fall, not to ignore the brutal severing of flesh from its lifeblood, but to accept that seasons shift, petals scatter, branches fracture, and the beauty we cling to is often the very thing that destroys us.

Suddenly

You left,
and suddenly
everything froze -
the sky locked in nightfall,
the earth steeped in petrichor,
and me draped in black,
following an empty hearse
to the funeral
of our fractured love.

Cut

I was taught
that if I carved away
enough of myself,
if I hollowed out this body,
someone whole
might make
a home here.

Flicker

As the sea
holds its tidal breath
and divides ocean from shore,
I choose a star,
a cavern of hidden sky
that might open somewhere dark.

I ask it for a spark,
a flicker, a light,
a whisper of hope
from its jar of lies,
just enough to ignite
a streetlight of memories
to guide me home, alone,
toward a dreaded tomorrow
I should never have
been left to face without you.

Worn Love Poems

All that remains of you
are the curled edges
of these worn love poems.

Moments your heart promised
to return to someday,
in a future you knew
was never meant to be.

How cruel,
to make me believe
I might be enough
to make you want to stay.

Death Notices

At times I feel
the only child
our love ever birthed
was a shadow
shaped like regret,
ironically named goodbye,
who died of wounds
from the knives
we buried between ribs,
as if watching it die
was our only mercy.

But if loving each other
was only agony,
why do I still see you
every time I return
to the scene of our crime?

Daisies

You let go of my hands,
so I used them to plant
daisies in your memory,
and watched as the heavens
watered them with my tears,
so I could lay them
at the foot of our grave,
the resting place
of my devotion.

I Am Not Okay

In fact, I am so far from it that the moon now touches me more intimately than the sun. I find safety in her choice not to expose my scars, shielding me with the gentle understanding she has long gifted to others like me, who once feared the dark.

I am learning to grow in her wake, allowing dusk to arrive without the stomach-knotting fear it once carried. I am healing; I am growing; I am basking in her beauty as if it were my chance to shine, my chance to live with the innocent abandon found in the darkest depths of night.

Less than Perfect Life

It is hard to admit,
but this less-than-perfect life
sometimes leaves me
homesick for death.

It leaves me wondering
what kind of prey
could be hungry enough
to devour me whole,
and then purge me,
like some forgotten disorder,
at the threshold of heaven or hell
(destination yet to be determined).

It leaves me wondering
if the Grim Reaper
would dance with me
beneath the broken streetlight,
or simply take me then and there,
without a whimper, without a word.

It's macabre, I know,
to admit that sometimes
this less-than-perfect life
leaves me homesick,
and longing for death.

Beautiful Destruction

Open the window of your rib cage and watch as I tear out your heart, an act of savage desire, my bloodied hands cradling the fragile pulse of your truth.

I'll lay bare your secrets, their jagged edges of vulnerability gleaming under stark light, each heartbeat pounding like a war drum, a death knell echoing through our silence.

This is the price of love - to expose what is fragile and broken, to linger in the shadows where we once dared to feel, where we stand naked and bleeding, witnesses to the chaos of desire, left grappling with the wreckage, the beautiful destruction of what we have become.

Not that I care

Not that I care, but I've noticed the afternoon shadows linger longer now. With precision they trace the outline of you across my bare skin, reminding me of what we shared: the warmth of your eyes, the softness of your smile, the way you held me, fragile as glass, until I was hemorrhaging amid the shattered remains.

Not that I care, but the nights stretch endlessly now, an embroidery of darkness stitched from longing, tears woven into a tapestry of unanswered questions. What hollowed space pulled you into that sullen, quiet abyss, leaving me shivering in a world without you?

I am Empty

I am empty, except for the cataclysmic trauma that coils around my shattered bones, seeps into my mind, and convinces me I am too damaged for this world.

I am empty, except for the bullets lodged in the pit of my stomach, each time you pulled my triggers just to watch me bleed.

I am empty, except for the vitriol of your words, the heaviness of your gaze, and the suffocating grip of your hands at my throat.

I am empty, except for the ghost of you and the broken remains of a life you methodically dismantled, piece by piece.

Caretaker of Sorrow

My heart is a graveyard, a vast, silent expanse of decay, where the ghosts of love and longing haunt the crumbling mausoleums of my memory.

In the darkness, I wander - lost and alone - searching for a way to escape the weight of my sorrow, yet every path leads only to more ruins, more rubble, more reminders of what has already been destroyed.

And still, I remain - a caretaker of sorrow - eternally bound to this graveyard heart, where the only thing more exhausting than the pain is the endless battle to forget.

Depressions Imprint

My body is a battlefield, imprinted with fallen soldiers, grenades in hand, scars tattooed against my skin; the wail of grieving loved ones, a sound unfamiliar even to God, now at home inside the war zone of my mind.

How do I make amends for a history I never wrote, yet bear the weight of guilt for? The bayonets and bullets may not have been mine, but the cemetery holding their ghosts could just as easily be.

Hashtag Movement

My skin crawls with the secrets of a hashtag movement, trauma carved into porcelain, fragile yet unyielding. The fractured hand of my own mind presses firmly across my mouth, as you would, an attempt to silence me, to ensure I would never utter *#MeToo* in a world so chaotic that voices dissolve in the rumble.

You didn't expect it, did you? The whisper that swelled slowly, deliberately into a scream. Can you still hear it, can you still feel the thump of my fists pounding against your chest in your two by three cell?

Do you understand now what it feels like to be held against your will?

Does it keep you awake at night, the way it does me?

Do you feel any remorse at all, or are you, too - like me - *#SorryNotSorry*?

I wonder if you lie awake, haunted by your choices, the weight of my truth pressing hard against your conscience.

Can you taste the bitterness of denial, the sharp edge of guilt, as you wrestle with the chaos you've sown?

#SorryNotSorry for the scars, for the screams, for the strength it took to rise, for the whispers that became a roar.

I am here – unbroken - and I will never be silenced again.

Intimate Darkness

You used my temple as an altar, the graze of your lips an unspoken prayer to the gods upon my skin.

You traced the smallest bruises on my hips, hidden in places no one else would look. Pressed into them with intent, your desire to reopen old wounds, the weight of your body pinning my silhouette to the sheets, a heaviness I have yet to escape.

After you left, the darkness felt more intimate than the light. My skin still burns from the absence of your touch, the absence of pain, the absence of anything except the truth that years later, I am still trying to scrub my memory clean of you.

Venom

I will never forget
the venom with which
you told me
my body
would never open
to the sun,
it would only
howl at the moon
until I became
just another
barren void
for your hate
to pour into.

This Rage is not Mine

Because I need to believe this rage is not mine, I will shed the skin I've outgrown, the same skin you caressed with a poisonous touch. I will scrub my flesh free of your lies, even when it leaves me exposed.

I will hold tightly to what's left of me, the precious pieces you could not touch. I'll bleed, I'll break, and I'll heal in the kindness and love you never gave.

Fire and Brimstone

I will never be that woman again, the one who let trauma ruin me while I used my shattered pieces to make you whole. Your lies did not deserve mending; they did not deserve the pieces of me you chose not to return.

Know this: I will not allow you to make me more callous nor will I let my sharp edges make me unworthy of love. Because of you, I am learning to forge a new self, tempered by fire and brimstone. I will no longer be defined by your lies.

Wailing Walls

I have forgotten
the safety of home,
of living within four walls
that do not wail at night.

Beneath a roof
that does not creak in rhythm
with every sob I exhale,
adorned with carpet
unstained by my blood.

Is this truly a home,
or a new kind of prison
conjured by trauma
my mind cannot release,
a place to which my body
still surrenders.

Fragile Architecture

The skeleton within me is a blueprint of bone and longing that aches with every heartbeat. It rattles like a mournful maraca in my chest, a haunting rhythm underscoring every step I take, every decision I make, every dream I chase.

I feel its presence most in the quiet moments, when my skin becomes a membrane stretched too thin, when I am painfully aware of the weight it bears; my deepest fears, my most fervent desires, my most impossible hopes.

It is the fragile architecture that holds me together, the delicate balance that keeps me from collapsing into dust.

Harpoon

Against my better judgement I pick apart lips sewn shut and let words I know will wound escape. I watch them find their marks like harpoons, breaking skin, piercing hearts, then hear the denials as they bleed before my eyes.

I am the monster with a warm heart and a kind smile, and against my better judgement, they still believe.

Toothpicks

I search for a home
in broken people,
picking apart their bones
like toothpicks,
exposing every tender morsel of pain
that has ever lived within them.

And then I wonder why
the jagged edges of their ribs
slice through my tender skin
when I try to find comfort
in their arms.

Things I Left Behind

Every version of myself that ever loved you, especially the one who believed you were all I deserved, who stitched violet into the fabric of my being, who braced broken bones with promises of "*never again.*"

I left behind your insecurities; I was never the one responsible for the blood-stained bruises. They were born of your so-called confusion, or perhaps more truthfully, your grand delusions.

I left behind the apologies, hollow words that caught in my throat, tumbling out whenever I needed to lie. How could I ever be sorry for what I hadn't done?

I left behind the monster and your suffocating shadow. Yet I will always carry the trauma, a relentless weight that anchors me to the past, a reminder of the truth I cannot escape.

Jagged Little Pill

The thing is, no one knows your pain, the shrillness of knives driven into bone, strumming every nerve like a frantic cellist. Back and forth, back and forth, demanding your body play a song it has never known, in a tempo it cannot possibly keep. A percussion ensemble thrums inside your skin... thrum... thrum... thrum.

The searing agony cuts like a record's needle played at double speed, deepening the grooves of madness. An incessant loop of a song you despise, refusing to leave you be.

Your only escape? The delirium of a jagged little pill, a bittersweet reprieve, a fleeting anesthesia that softens the torment, until you cannot tell if you are lost or if you have finally been found.

Aftermath of Goodbye

In the aftermath of goodbye, your absence seeps into the grain of familiar things, discolouring memories like light on empty spaces, shifting their weight.

Loss becomes a shape I learn to navigate, a hollow in the air where you used to be, where loneliness settles against my skin, slowly reshaping me.

In this void, a new pulse unfurls, where presence and absence entwine, and I trace the contours of your loss, finding both strange peace and melancholy beauty in the silence that remains.

Foresight

The smugness of foresight rests on my tongue like a bruise. I've been here before, the ache of being right when no one cared to listen, the bitter familiarity of knowing the shape of what's to come, bound to watch as others stumble into it.

The weight of unheeded warnings press heavy in my chest, a silence gathering like storm clouds on the horizon. All I can do is hold my tongue and let the lessons unfold.

Your Mouth is a Grave

Your mouth is a grave for my name. Buried in dirt and filth, I rot slowly, a corpse in your narrative. Your degradation, gnaws at my flesh, promising I'll die of self-loathing long before your hate has the chance to kill me.

Smothered Skies

Please hold your tongue.
Do not speak of all
your hopes and fragile dreams,
for nothing good can grow
beneath these smothered skies.

Better to wait until words
are no longer ours to utter,
and leave them instead
as flowers upon my grave.

Death Comes

Death comes for me, bare teeth gnashing, salivating at the thought of another notch on its belt.

It waits at my empty grave, leaning against the tombstone where my name is already carved, picking its teeth with the bones of those who went before me.

Who am I to argue? It comes for us all, sooner or later, it is the *sooner* that unsettles me, the thought that no matter how tightly I cling to life, how fiercely I resist, death may well have the last laugh.

When it comes, know I did not yield. Even the bravest heart must, one day, surrender to the dark.

Enveloped

The sea's dark flesh yielded beneath my fingertips like damp earth, kelp's rubbery fronds coiling around my ankles as I waded into the surge, where barnacles etch the rocks with time's embrace.

It tasted of nostalgia and pain, the brackish flavor of a childhood shoreline where river and sea entwined.

The salt sting upon my lips carried me back to weathered pilings, to the rope's creak beneath a dock's slow sway, a symphony of memory echoing in the salt-kissed air.

This was the moment my past enveloped me, and I did not resist its pull.

Bring Me

Bring me all your tomorrows, blurred by tears, the ones you fear you'll never reach through grief, those filled with love, laughter, hope, and all you imagine will never return.

Bring me your apologies, Plant them deep at the foot of my grave and let me nourish them, for it is never too late to grow something beautiful from this pain.

Bring me purple wisteria. Let it veil my name beneath its fragrant petals as it climbs my headstone. Know that I am forever held in nature's embrace.

Bring me all of your tears, so the wash of your ocean may be the last thing I feel, ebbing softly against my skin.

And then bring me your promise: your solemn vow to forget me, to forget all that we were.

Please - never visit again.

Tenacity

These shadows claw at the door,
begging to return to their bones.

I'll admit that I envy their tenacity
their unwavering ability
to endure the dark.

I confess, I am jealous
of the strange beauty
in their loneliness,
and the way they survive
this bleak life, alone.

Daggered Rain

Beneath the daggered rain,
a rift of leaves carries my cries
until they grow sodden,
soaked to the bone,
long before they ever reach the ears
of a single soul who could save me.

Bruise of Fate

A vase of wilted
purple pansies
adorns the grave
where your tender lips
once buried me.

You were always
the bruise of fate
that never fades away.

Requiem

I don't listen to the radio anymore,
it always ends in tears.
The soft tempo of my heart,
beating in time with our song,
becomes my only saviour
from the lyrical massacre
of the requiem for our dead love.

The Ghost of You

Lock the door behind you. I'm trying to keep the ghost of you from crawling back into my skin. Your touch lingers like a bruise, aching to be felt again. But I will not let you in, no more hauntings, no more late-night calls twisting like barbed wire around my heart.

I will burn the photographs, shatter the memories, and dance in the ashes, because this time, I refuse to be your ghost.

Grim Reaper

How blessed we are
to be filled
with such heartbreak
that the ruins
of these two
abandoned hearts
can write,
with their silence
the reaper's
favourite poem.

In Loving Memory

In loving memory of the poet within, the woman who wrapped words around her wrists to stem the bleeding and yet still faltered; who let the world into her heart, and watched them break it; who believed that purging the essence of her being could transform her into more than mere lyrics with no melody; who never lived long enough to know if anything she wrote found its way into the crevice of another soul, or if it even mattered at all.

Mortal Wound

Slain bodies pile up,
blood red like autumn leaves,
seeping into the earth,
staining the ground.
I search every inch of my body
for bullet holes,
for the mortal wound
that could end this aching,
hollowed-out despair,
only to find nothing changes,
hope is still a sniper
with poor aim.

Glimpses from the Abyss

Ampersands

I am the burnt-umber
edges of Autumn,
a funeral song,
an unfinished epitaph,
the glassy blur of teary eyes
that cannot cry enough
to soothe this grief

I am a broken crucifix
in the hands of an unfair god,
the mo(u)rning after trauma,
an empty space
between and after ampersands.

I am rain, falling, fallen,
silence after a storm.
I am a shadow in the dark,
one light never manages to find.

I am love, erased,
not by all that I am,
but all that I will never be.

Starkness

Open wounds,
raw and unassured,
reveal what lies beneath
not just pain:
but the weight of untold stories.

A space where healing feels foreign,
where every breath stings,
as if to mark the depth
of what we try to forget.

In this moment,
there is no grace,
only the starkness of being,
the truth of existence laid bare.

Fragile Glass

I gather moments like fragile glass, holding them tightly, their colours dancing like crimson sunsets, watching their sheen fade.

Memories grow heavier by the day, until they are nothing more than a collection of echoes, whispers, fleeting smiles, and moments I can't take back, tethered to a time I can't reclaim.

Then comes the inevitable crack, and I am left with shards, the beauty of their fragility, a reminder of all I dared to love.

Sculptor

She sculpts him from the stars;
he whittles her from trees.
If they were made to be together,
their love would last eternity.
Instead the stars will fall,
the trees die of old age.
and love becomes a fairytale,
you read upon this page.

Barefoot Girl

I haven't swum in years,
but now I have no choice
but to take the leap
to save a drowning soul,
her calm reflection,
hiding a frantic fight
beneath the surface,
just out of reach
of the barefoot girl
who once believed
this ocean was the freedom
that would save her.

Cradling Hour

In this fragile hour,
I learn to cradle sorrow,
to let it fill the spaces,
and find the beauty
in the ache of remembering.

One Point Three Light Seconds

You instill in me the notion
that in every moment
we are never more
than one point three
light-seconds
from the same moon,

Never has something
so comforting
felt so utterly
out of reach.

August Rush

Open the door to your heart;
let me search for your smile
and those eyes that smolder
in the wintery depths
like an August rush.

Let me touch the moonlight
of your heart and will you back to life.

Tell me this is a dream,
a masquerade
of love that has simply
forgotten how to breathe,
or watch me fade
into the crook of your arm,
now lifeless and cold,
a broken shell
of the girl you once knew.

If You Asked

If you asked me how I'm doing, I might speak of the weight of silence, how it settles in corners like dust on forgotten shelves.

I could share the warmth of morning light, how it breaks through the window settling on the wings of glass butterflies, a gentle reminder that the world still turns even when I feel frozen.

But perhaps I'd simply smile, a fleeting moment of happiness, because some days, the question itself is enough.

Robins

Where do robins go
when the earth cries?
Do they seek shelter
beneath the groan
of ancient branches,
find haven within
umber hollows of sturdy oaks,
or do they simply dance
in the tears of heaven
and sing a song of hope
for better days.

#MeToo

In the pause between words, where courage trembles,
a wave stirs, tsunami whispers unfolding,
stories hidden, heavy with unspoken weight.

Each click sparks the night ablaze; voices intertwine, lifting
the veil, secrecy unravelling thread by thread, shame's fragile
fabric laid bare.

A chorus of truths emerges, heartbreak and triumph
entwined, whispers swelling into roars, power reclaimed,
strength found in shared truth.

We rise, a collective heartbeat, pulsating with each refrain,
every secret a story, every story a ripple healing the world
with each daring voice that speaks *#MeToo*.

Wander

I wander to a place where names dissolve into thin air, a landscape untouched by another's memory, where the imprint of my footsteps carries no weight, and the horizon stretches endlessly into the unknown.

Here, I become a whisper, a moment lost in the folds of time, where the sun paints shadows that have never learned my shape.

Breath, a soft departure, a gentle retreat into the unfamiliar, where the past sheds its skin and the future waits, welcoming me to dance in anonymity, to exist simply as a note in a song no one will ever hear.

Unmet Hopes

In the stillness of unmet hopes, disappointment unfurls like a withered leaf, soft and haunting.

We craft our dreams with delicate hands, only to watch them slip, like sand through our fingers, each grain a sigh of unuttered longing.

Here in the quiet aftermath, we discover the art of disappointment, a bittersweet acceptance that becomes a canvas, waiting for new colours to shape beauty from our scars.

If Nothing Goes to Plan

If nothing goes to plan, take my trembling and make it your own, mould my softness into something beautiful, someone less like me and more like someone you could love.

Kiss me softly, so I can no longer taste regret on your lips, or the blame that sits atop your tongue, waiting for an escape.

Trace the outline of us, the silhouette that exists in those final moments of dark before the light, find perfection in our imperfections, and if nothing goes to plan,

love me anyway.

Wrong About Love

I was wrong about love, believing it arrived like a storm, all thunder and light, a sudden rush of warmth on a midsummer's night.

Instead, it whispers, soft as a breaking dawn, revealing itself in quiet, tender moments: your hand brushing against mine, the smile on your lips when you say my name, the weight of comfortable silence.

It grew roots beneath the surface, not all at once, but through a slow, steady bloom, in happiness, in tears, thriving in spaces between words, where the true understanding of love came to light, came to life, became ours to protect at all cost from a cold and dispassionate world.

How to Be a Stranger

Embrace the silence. Wander streets unnoticed, eyes lowered, as the familiar fades into the distance.

Learn the art of vanishing in plain sight, becoming a ghost in a crowded room. Discover the peace of eating alone, lost in the hum of whispered stories.

Carry your own world. Listen deeply to the rustle of leaves. Balance the weight of unspoken words. Find beauty in fleeting moments.

A quiet breath in a noisy city, a soft smile offered to a passerby, an understanding that sometimes, being a stranger is a beautiful freedom few will ever know.

Judgement

Before you decide to cast the first stone,
pause in the silence, feel the weight alone.
Before you presume to know all that's true,
sift through the shadows and consider the view.

Before you cut down hopes of the unheard,
take a moment to question, to listen, to learn.
Before hearing both sides is a choice that you make,
remember the stories that linger and ache.

In the rush to decide, we often forget,
the truth wears many faces, its depth a deep net.
So please, hold your judgment, let empathy lead,
in the dance of discourse, find solace and heed.

For beyond reasonable doubt lies the heart of the matter,
where understanding blooms and compassion won't shatter.
In the tapestry of voices, we weave our shared fate,
let us seek true connection before it's too late.

Lie to Me

If you must lie, tell me we'll survive this. Tell me the distance between us doesn't exist, that in this world, every glance still feels like home.

When you look at me, tell me you see the woman you loved, not her fractured shell, cracked and fragile as glass.

Tell me I'm beautiful, and I'll lie, say I believe you, though the scars etched in my bones, whisper otherwise.

Tell me you love me, more than life itself, more than the stars love the moon, more fiercely than waves crash upon the shore. And I'll tell you I feel it, even in the silence between us.

Tell me you hold all the pieces of my heart, that it isn't impossible to make me whole again, like a puzzle, waiting for your hands.

Tell me this time you'll stay, and I will lie, and promise I will too.

Poems by the River

I fold poems by the river,
leave origami sonnets
clinging to the banks
among the reeds.

The sun inhales
hopeful haiku,
exhales all the tenderness,
my heart can bestow
into a world
still desperately
craving love.

Search Engine

By the glow of the screen, my search history unfolds, a puzzle of unspoken pain, scattered pieces, a whisper of fragile strength, a quest for answers to battles fought in silence.

I type *healing, support,* walking the edges of anguish and survival, shadows of a past that lingers still. Each click a step toward reclaiming my voice, my body, myself.

Survivor stories, my trembling hands search, yearning for connection in this isolating world. I find solace in shared truths, reminders that this fight is not mine alone.

In the shadows of *how to cope,* I uncover resilience, the courage to confront, to breathe, to gather the pieces of my spirit, protecting the flickering light within.

This is my search history, a chronicle of healing, a declaration - I am still here. Still fighting. Transformed by the flames of my story, growing stronger, brighter, and one day, I will be able to say it plainly, unbroken and unapologetically me.

A Single Shoe

In the quiet of an empty room, a single shoe rests beneath the bed, laces frayed, toe scuffed with stories untold. Echoes of tiny laughter linger in the air; memories tucked into corners the sunlight barely reaches.

Dust dances in the stillness, whispers of footsteps now gone. The marks on the floor tell of growing, of learning, of leaving, while the walls hold their breath, patient and watchful, waiting for a voice to fill the void, for someone long gone to finally find their way back home.

Tap Dancing Sunflowers

It is always in the moments
of my own decay
that I find beauty,
sunflowers tap dance
on a windowsill stage,
against the rounded shoulders
of sunlit hills at dawn.

But never in the fading reflection
of the woman God forgot.

Farewell to A Year

I hope you are not beneath the setting sun, waiting for the warm summer breeze to blow us back to the way things were, to places we can never return to. We both know the only parts of us that ever fell in love were our flaws, and the deep-seated rust from an endless sea spray of tears.

You kept me on my knees; head bowed in prayer or despair. And while I am grateful for the glimmers of hope you gave the small miracles you offered, it is time for me to stand, to bask in tomorrow because living as the hostage to your heart is no life at all.

Please don't think I me ungrateful, or hateful, for the burden you laid on my shoulders, for the darkness you pressed into my soul in anticipation of my fall. Know this: I simply learned to befriend my demons, to love them into invisibility, much like myself.

So I bid thee farewell. This is where we say Goodbye. Farewell. So long, old friend.

And that sunset you see, the brilliance of tangerine and gold, it is me smiling in delight, that you finally love me enough to leave.

Bare-Hearted Fool

I am a bare-hearted fool,
not the kind
who wears love on my sleeve,
but the kind
who carves love letters into my skin
for all of the world to see.

I bleed poetry from every crevice,
yet cannot bear to watch you
try to stem the bleeding,
to save me from myself.

I'm a survivor, by definition,
still kicking, still screaming
my way through trauma,
lifting my heart
from of the abyss,
only to be drained
of every last drop.

And still, I rise,
the words spill,
the poems bleed,
and I will continue to speak
the only language I know,
the language of vulnerability.

Becoming

In the morning's hush,
a bud begins to unfurl,
releasing whispers
of colour into the soft light.

Each petal slowly reveals
edges tender and uncertain.

In this quiet unfolding,
the beauty of becoming takes shape,
a gentle infusion of light and shadow,
form and meaning.

The bud's transformation
proves the gentle power of growth,
reminding us that beauty lies not in being,
but in becoming.

Without Poetry, Who am I?

I am a murmur in the dark, a sound that never quite becomes a voice, a presence felt but never defined, a shape vague and hard to hold, a series of impressions, smudges on the page refusing to take on a clear form.

But poetry is the spark that sets my thoughts ablaze, the fire that sharpens my words. With it, I am unbound – thoughts and words a riot of sound and sense, a fusion of broken pieces, a collage of contradictions; a voice that is all at once fragmented yet whole.

Poetry Saved Me

Poetry saved me, not in grand gestures and fame, but in quiet moments, a line that stopped me mid-thought, a breath caught in ink, where chaos yielded clarity and my sorrow found its voice.

In the margins of sleepless nights, where shadows danced on the walls, verses became lifelines, each stanza a step toward hope, each verse a refuge, reminding me I was never alone in the depths of my own making.

Once, in the stillness, a poem whispered my name, revealing secrets I dared not speak. And in that moment, I learned to weave my pain into beauty, to transform despair into light, to find solace in my own stories, in the quiet assurance that my heart holds the words to guide me home.

Let Your Lies be Lanterns

Lie to me, whisper sweet untruths that dance like shadows across the walls of my mind, carving comfort from the chaos as the world spins, unraveled and unpredictable.

Tell me the stars are always within reach, that hope is a garden tenderly kept, where weeds are only memories of yesterday's storms.

Wrap my heart in silk; let your words be a balm, a fragile facade against the raw edges of reality, where truth cuts, sharp as winter's breath.

In the quiet of night, when the moon hangs heavy, let your lies be lanterns, guiding me through the labyrinth of dreams, where I may believe in the beauty of the unreal.

Winter's Embrace

All I wish is to be a whisper of autumn, crisp air carrying the scent of fallen leaves, a fleeting presence, unbound by the weight of time.

To blend with gold and russet, to dance in twilight, where shadows stretch long and the world softens.

To be the quiet before the first frost, the soft sigh of trees shedding their burdens, inviting stillness, a gentle pause.

In this season of release, I long to embody the grace, to find beauty in transition, to be the calm before winter's embrace.

The Scars I Carry

The scars I carry tell the story of love. They are not blemishes, but whispers of us, etched into the hills and valleys of my skin.

Here, where your fingertips traced a path, a faint line remains, a memory of the night we danced beneath the stars, our laughter echoing through the empty streets.

This small crescent moon near my wrist, recalls the time we fell, scraped knees, tear-stained cheeks, yet our hands clasped tight, a silent promise of forever.

And this one, hidden beneath my ribs, a secret only you know, a mark of the pain we endured, the strength we found in each other's arms, a testament to the depth of our love.

These are not imperfections, my darling, but constellations of our love, proof of the life we've built, a love story written not on paper, but inscribed like ink upon the canvas of our hearts.

Caught in the Fray

I am a leaf caught in the fray,
tangled in life's tapestry,
precariously poised between
the safety of woven silk strands
and the precipice of extinction,
a single breath away
from being forgotten,
or perhaps never existing at all.

Such is the delicate balance
of life.

Ode to Grief

In sorrow's dark and lonely night,
grief creeps, a thief, and steals away
The warmth of love, the light of sight,
leaving only emptiness to stay.

With heavy heart and tears that flow,
grief whispers secrets, cold and grey.
A lonely path that few may know,
through shadows cast, it leads the way.

Time may loosen grief's tight chains,
but memories of joy remain,
A sorrow that will never wane.
even broken hearts survive the pain.

Tremble

This moment trembles
with potential,
a fracture in the ordinary.
I seize the jagged edge
and tear the future open.

The sound of my heartbeat,
the only truth I need.
I am the reckoning,
I am the storm,
and the time is now.

Luminous Hearts

Matriarch (For Tick)

She carries within her
whispers of dawn's
soft embrace,
her smile ascends,
emerging; a sunrise
unearthed from her soul
to illuminate the shadows
of ochre hollows.

From her gaze to her bare feet,
the shadows she casts
sway in a gentle rhythm,
keeping time
with the softness
of her ebb and flow.

She is nothing less
than captivating
an ethereal testament
to the wisdom
and sacred guidance
of her earth's
one true matriarch
the Mother of Nature.

Band of Brothers (For Baz)

A band of brothers is not always born of blood
they are discovered in the hills and valleys of life,
over land and sea, beneath sun and stars,
forged in darkness yet fuelled by light,
laughter, and love.

This band of brothers forged
a bond of indestructible steel,
hardened hearts with a softness reserved only
for the company of each other.

Today one of the mighty has fallen,
into arms not meant to be, not now, not yet.
Though they kneel for a fallen friend,
there is only one way to honour him
and that is to rise together,
shoulder to shoulder, arm in arm,
a conflagration of phoenix
ascending from the ashes of love.

For the bond of brothers
is never truly broken,
never fractured, never lost.
It withstands even death
and lives eternal in laughter,
in the montage of memories
and in the hearts of brothers
not born of blood
but by choice.

Scrubs (haiku For Nurse Ryan)

in scrubs, they bring light,
compassion woven through care,
nurses, heroes' grace.

To the Man Who Loved Me First
(For Gramps)

The ocean sings your name, a siren call drawing me home to endless horizons, where pink-fairy floss clouds melt into the cerulean embrace of the sea. The rhythm of the waves whisper secrets of our past, a reminder of each tear you once brushed away.

It is here, I see you most vividly, your crooked captain's hat perched atop your furrowed brow, a whistle poised on your lips, a rendition of *"Oh, What a Beautiful Morning"* just a smile away. I remember golden afternoons, the sun scattering sparkles across the water as you taught me to navigate the tides. Your laughter was the wind at my back, urging me forward, a little girl who grew sea legs just to dance with the waves, just to see you smile.

The scent of salt and sun-kissed skin lingers in my memory, echoing the warmth of your embrace. I can almost hear the gulls overhead, their cries mingling with your voice, guiding me home.

Now, standing on the shoreline, I reflect on what it means to be loved, wholly, completely. Though tides may shift and the winds may change, your love remains a beacon, lighting my way.

Golden Cradle (For My Soulmate)

I can always see
pastel sunsets
resting in his smile
a golden cradle
upon which
laughter sleeps.

Like moonlight
refracting off a still ocean,
his joy bends light itself.

A daily eclipse
as dusk kneels
upon the altar
      of his smile.

ABOUT THE AUTHOR

Karen Richards resides in Australia, and she is a writer of poetry and prose, the author of four other poetry collections ***The Hollowed Edge of Almost, Release the Fireflies, Wrapped in Folds of Midnight*** and ***The Way My Words Fall***.

Karen has been writing poetry for 35 years and enjoys connecting with her audience with emotion and simplicity through shared experiences. Her poetry has also been featured in many anthologies over the past six years.

Karen currently writes to a social media audience, and her work can be found on Instagram, Threads and Substack.

www.ingramcontent.com/pod-product-compliance
Lightning Source LLC
Chambersburg PA
CBHW031248290426
44109CB00012B/491